INTRODUCTION

"I had spent 35 years trying to have, do, and be everything I could. I had been a good mother, good boss, good wife, good daughter, good role model—and now I know I was good and miserable."

This quote comes from the book *Enough Is Enough*. It was written by Carol Osborn who founded Superwomen's Anonymous, a self-help group for overachieving women that guarantees no meetings, classes, or fundraisers.

When the "second wave" of feminism in the 1960s opened more opportunities for women, many of us embraced the new challenge. We believed we could do it all. We thought we could have endless physical and psychic energy, careers, marriage, children, and exciting love lives that provided tantalizing material for romance novels. We could not only do what men do, we could do more than what men do.

The recessions of the 1970s brought more women—those who had worked in more traditional homemaking roles—into the paid labor although political and economic conditions revolutionized our lives, domestic conditions stayed mostly the same.

It can seem that having it all means doing it all. We wrestle with the "second shift"—work we have to do at home after completing the first shift at the office. This double duty forces us into roles of Superwomen, leaving many of us ineffective and exhausted.

Today we are becoming more attuned to the importance of wellness and health prevention. This revealing book tells us how to conquer the daily challenges that women encounter at home and work. The first section offers sensible success strategies to help with family relationships and guidelines for parenting and understanding aging parents. It also offers tips for better organization, vacations, financial health, and friendships. The following sections give wellness strategies, easy-to-understand information about diseases that sometimes afflict women, and action plans to implement the success and wellness strategies. Workshops are given throughout the book to help identify concerns and problems.

Health Strategies for Working Women is written for all women who want to be successful and feel great. Welcome to the adventure!

Merlene T. Sherman

CONTENTS

INTRODUCTION i

SECTION I   SUCCESS STRATEGIES 1

Power-Organizing 4
Power-Organizing Strategies 4

Telephone Timesavers 7
Telephone Strategies 7

Work Alternatives 8
Work Alternative Strategies 8

Vacations, Weekends, and Holidays 11
Personal-Time Strategies 12

Women and Money 13
Financial Health Workshop 13
Financial Health Strategies 14

Single Working Women 17
Single Women's Success Strategies 18

Harassment 19
Overcoming Harassment 20

Marriage 21
Household-Work Cooperation 21
Marriage Strategies Workshop 22

Healthy Pregnancy 23
Workplace Pregnancy Policies 23
Healthy Baby Strategies 24

Parenting 27
Make Room For Daddy 28
Parental Pointers 29
The Parent Track 30
Making Time Count Strategies 30

Single Parents 31
Single Parent Strategies 31

Aging Parents 33
The Sandwich Generation 33
Caregiving Strategies 34

Women's Friendships and Health 35
Men's and Women's Friendships: The Differences 35
Workplace Friendships 36
Friendship Strategies 36
Get-Together Strategies 37

CONTENTS (Continued)

SECTION II   WELLNESS STRATEGIES 39

    Sleep, Wonderful Sleep...................................41
        Reasons Why We Don't Sleep 42
        Sleep Strategies...................................43

    Vim, Vigor, and Vital Exercise...................................45
        Calorie Burning Workshop 46
        When and Where to Exercise 47
        Exercise Strategies 47

    Eating Right 49
        Iron Watch 49
        Eating Strategies 50

    Battle of the Bulge...................................51
        Weight Control Strategies 52

    Storm Clouds of Smoke 53
        Ponder These Pluses 53
        The Bad News Gets Worse 53
        Smoking Workshop 54

    That Keyed-Up Feeling 57
        Burn-Out Workshop 58
        Stress-Busting Strategies 59

    Seek Solitude 61
        Solitude Strategies 62

SECTION III   KNOW YOUR BODY 63

    The Body's Timeclock 65
        Personal Cycle Log Workshop 66

    #1 Killer of Women 67
        Risk Factors That You Can't Change 68
        The Working Woman's Heart 68
        Heart Workshop 69
        Healthy Heart Strategies 69

    Breast Cancer 71
        Breast Cancer Prevention Strategies 71

    Osteoporosis...................................73
        Osteoporosis Workshop 74
        Strategies to Prevent and Treat Osteoporosis 75

SECTION IV   CONCLUSION 77
    Action Strategies 79

RESOURCES 81

HEALTH STRATEGIES FOR WORKING WOMEN

Merlene T. Sherman

A FIFTY-MINUTE™ SERIES BOOK

CRISP PUBLICATIONS, INC.
Menlo Park, California

HEALTH STRATEGIES FOR WORKING WOMEN

Merlene T. Sherman

CREDITS
Editor: **Kay Kepler**
Layout and Composition: **Interface Studio**
Cover Design: **Carol Harris**
Artwork: **Ralph Mapson**

Copyright © 1991 by Crisp Publications, Inc.
Printed in the United States of America

English language Crisp books are distributed worldwide. Our major international distributors include:

CANADA: Reid Publishing, Ltd., Box 69559—109 Thomas St., Oakville, Ontario Canada L6J 7R4. TEL: (416) 842-4428; FAX: (416) 842-9327

AUSTRALIA: Career Builders, P.O. Box 1051, Springwood, Brisbane, Queensland, Australia 4127. TEL: 841-1061, FAX: 841-1580

NEW ZEALAND: Career Builders, P.O. Box 571, Manurewa, Auckland, New Zealand. TEL: 266-5276, FAX: 266-4152

JAPAN: Phoenix Associates Co., Mizuho Bldg. 2-12-2, Kami Osaki, Shinagawa-Ku, Tokyo 141, Japan. TEL: 3-443-7231, FAX: 3-443-7640

Selected Crisp titles are also available in other languages. Contact International Rights Manager Suzanne Kelly at (415) 323-6100 for more information.

Library of Congress Catalog Card Number 90-83482
Sherman, Merlene T.
Health Strategies for Working Women
ISBN 1-56052-079-5

This book is printed on recyclable paper with soy ink.

S E C T I O N

I

Success Strategies

SUCCESSFUL OUTCOMES

The world is filled with people who are biding their time and looking for the brass ring. They are waiting for something extraordinary to occur so they can become successful. Unfortunately, that's not the way that success happens.

Success doesn't come from sitting on your hands. It comes from the recognition of opportunity and a steadfast determination to turn that opportunity into a reward.

This section of *Health Strategies for Working Women* gives you an opportunity to learn about important strategies that will lead you to successful outcomes. You'll discover strategies that are adaptable to your lifestyle and tactics that will make the strategies easy to implement. You'll also find "Vital Signs" that provide fun and fascinating facts to help you make the strategies work.

Don't just twiddle your thumbs. Go for it and seize this opportunity. Remember, there is no predictability on earth—only opportunity!

POWER-ORGANIZING

VITAL SIGNS—*Power-Organizing*

- Each hour in your life makes a difference. The average American spends six years waiting—for airplanes, at the cash register—including six months waiting for lights to turn green.
- ''No'' is the most dynamic timesaver in the English language.

Get control of your life by power-organizing. Concentrate your time on things that are most important to you. When you try to do too much, you clutter your life and don't have time to do what really matters. When you power-organize, you feel in control and are healthier.

POWER-ORGANIZING STRATEGIES

The power-organized working woman arranges her schedule to get the most out of each day. Four strategies for power-organizing involve setting priorities, planning your days, using time efficiently, and uncluttering.

STRATEGY #1—Setting priorities.

- Make time to do the things you value and love. Invite a friend for a Saturday sandwich. Take your child to the park.

- Weed out and don't buy unessential items. The more things you have, the more time it takes to keep them.

- Set aside specific times each day. A working woman needs time to relax, think, and renew.

- Take time for things high on your priority list. As one organizing expert claims, ''If you don't think you have time for it, you probably need it more than the rest of us!''

STRATEGY #2—Planning your days.

No one likes a disorderly, rumpled life. It generates confusion, makes you less productive, and saps the energy you need for good physical and mental health.

Try these four planning ideas to coordinate your life:

- Forget the idea that doing more is doing better. Schedule only what you can realistically do. The person who completes ten tasks instead of five does not win a gold star, particularly when those jobs aren't done well.

- Double the time that you think a project will take. Interruptions, emergencies, and unforeseen tasks inevitably arise.

- Use a planner with reminders and daily and weekly plans to schedule your time.

  Long-term reminders. Plan things such as next month's dental appointments. Keep back-up projects on this list.

  Short-term reminders. Plan tasks that you need to do during the month.

  Weekly plan. Make a weekly plan that allows you to pace yourself and avoid the frustration of trying to accomplish everything on Monday. Research shows that you relieve stress the most when you do this Sunday night.

  Daily plan. Add yesterday's unfinished tasks and priority items for the day. Consolidate messages, reminders, and phone calls and make a fresh ''do it'' list daily. Limit the tasks so that you can be flexible.

- Set aside a few minutes each day for reflection and planning. The time between awakening in the morning and the start of your day may be the only time that you're undisturbed and alone.

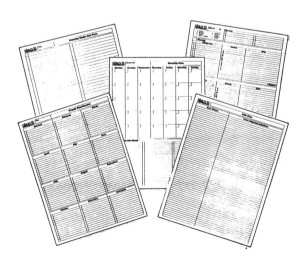

POWER STRATEGIES (Continued)

STRATEGY #3—Using time efficiently.

Starting and Stopping

Working in spurts takes more time than working straight through because restarting takes time. If you must quit work on a project for several hours, try to stop at an interesting part. When you begin again, you'll get a fast start because you won't dread resuming the project.

However, most people can't effectively concentrate more than an hour in one sitting. Take short breaks to relieve stress, but avoid long layoffs.

Waiting time

When you're driving or stuck in traffic, use these suggestions to spend time productively:

- Listen to tapes of books, old radio shows, or self-improvement programs while you drive.
- Read, write, or work on projects when you are stopped.
- Give yourself a breather. Sometimes relaxing is the best use of waiting time.

STRATEGY #4—Uncluttering.

- File, don't pile. Throw away old letters, mail, catalogs, and reports.
- Do only one thing at a time. Put away items that you won't use within three hours.
- Straighten your work space and rooms at home before leaving or going to bed.

When you power-organize, remember that perfectionism is a time-robber. Identify the point of diminishing returns and learn to live with some loose ends.

TELEPHONE TIME-SAVERS

VITAL SIGNS—Telephone

- **The typical household generates 3.5 calls a day lasting an average of 6.17 minutes each.**
- **Of the people who own answering machines, more than one-third use them to screen calls.**

Humorist Erma Bombeck once announced that if she had to choose between having another baby and another phone, she'd take the child without question!

TELEPHONE STRATEGIES

Telephone calls can disrupt schedules, meals, conversations, and meetings. That's why it's important to develop time-saving strategies to make that electronic miracle a bearable convenience.

TELEPHONE STRATEGY 1—Do double-duty.

Read, file, or write when you are waiting for a person to answer the phone. Mend clothes or manicure your nails when you talk on the phone at home.

TELEPHONE STRATEGY 2—Plan phone time.

Set aside one or two time periods for calls each day. You'll be more effective with other tasks that you don't interrupt.

TELEPHONE STRATEGY 3—Leave specific messages.

State a time when you can call back or take a return call. Give the purpose of your call when leaving a business message.

TELEPHONE STRATEGY 4—Cultivate conversation shorteners.

When you have time restraints, use these ideas to warn callers that your time is limited.

- "It sounds fascinating, but I only have a few minutes."
- "Before we hang up..."

TELEPHONE STRATEGY 5—Don't answer.

You aren't obligated to answer your phone when it rings at an inconvenient time. Unplug the phone or buy an answering machine if you can't stand to hear it ring. (Warning: You may discourage friends if you're too unavailable.)

TELEPHONE STRATEGY 6—Cut short conversations with annoying salespeople.

You throw away "junk mail." Throw away "junk calls." Don't worry about hurting the salesperson's feelings. Rejection is part of a salesperson's job.

TELEPHONE STRATEGY 7—Get the facts.

Write down the person's name and extension when you place an order, request service, or follow-up on a problem. You'll save time and frustration later on.

WORK ALTERNATIVES

VITAL SIGNS—Work Alternatives

- **The contingent work force of part-timers, temporaries, and freelancers is growing more rapidly than the conventional work force.**
- **A recent study indicates that flextime reduced tardiness in 42% of the companies surveyed, elevated morale in 39% and improved productivity in 33%.**

Family concerns are changing the way jobs, benefits, and careers are structured. Flexible work schedules, family leave, child and elder care options, and alternative career paths are becoming more common and helping women stay healthy.

WORK ALTERNATIVE STRATEGIES

The following section describes some of the work alternatives that are available to women. If those that would suit you are not available at your workplace, perhaps you could help implement them.

#1—Flextime.

Carol Smith is at home with her three young children when they meet the morning school bus. She has chosen a flextime schedule at her job to accommodate her children's schedules. Carol benefits from her company's staggered scheduling by working from 10:00 a.m. to 6:00 p.m.

Other workers in Carol's company have chosen 7:00 a.m. to 3:00 p.m. schedules. A few employees have opted to work ten-hour days, four days a week.

Flextime scheduling allows Sarah to leave work an hour early each Tuesday to take her daughter to piano lessons. She makes up her time on Wednesdays.

Some companies plan the year's work, prorate pay, and use flextime schedules to let employees vary their working times. Employees can work longer hours during the school year and take more time off in the summer when their kids are home.

Other flextime variations let employees reduce their schedules and salaries to take shorter work days or weeks, take off blocks of time, or occasionally take time off.

#2—Flexspace.

Flexspace is the concept of the 90s. Employees communicate with their offices via computer and work at home part or all of the week. Both employer and worker benefit. ''I can take care of my son, walk the dog, and wear comfortable clothes while working at my own pace,'' notes one woman who is a flexspace employee. And the company reaps the benefit of a happier, motivated, and more productive employee.

#3—Job-sharing.

The job-sharing flextime concept lets two employees arrange their hours to provide full work coverage and divide the responsibilities and compensation of one job. Janet teaches Mondays and Tuesdays, and Helen teaches the same class Thursdays and Fridays. They alternate on Wednesdays.

Both women job-share for different reasons. Job-sharing is crucial for Janet because she needs time to care for her elderly parents and still be Mom to four teenagers. Job-sharing allows Helen to study at the university and do volunteer work at the zoo.

#4—Part-time work.

Part-time, temporary, and freelance work is booming. Some women use part-time work as a way to ease their transition from homemaking. Others want to enter and stay in the working world as part-timers.

A small factory in St. Paul, Minnesota has a part-time ''mothers' shift.'' Women see their kids off in the morning during the school year and work from 8:30 a.m. to 2:00 p.m. During the summer, they work from 7:00 a.m. to noon and spend afternoons with their children.

#5—Family leave.

Paid and unpaid time off for births, adoptions, or care of sick children, spouses, and parents is becoming more widespread in the workplace. Many companies are experimenting with ways to give working parents or those with elderly relatives more time off. And more state laws are protecting employee leaves of absence.

WORK ALTERNATIVES (Continued)

> #6—Child Care.

We live in a country that upholds the mothering image but makes it difficult for a family to live on one income. Recognizing this working mother's dilemma, more employers are providing support services such as child care to help their employees balance work and parenting.

Some businesses provide daycare centers; others offer child care financial assistance to neighborhood centers or dependent-care spending accounts to employee parents. Some companies provide child care information and advice, or help workers find child or elder care. (For more information about flexible work options, see the resource section of this book.)

VACATIONS, WEEKENDS, AND HOLIDAYS

VITAL SIGNS—Vacations

- **Renting a vacation house is often more private and less expensive than traditional hotel accommodations.**
- **Active holidays can be as renewing as stress-free time away from the job. A different experience like wilderness backpacking can refresh and clear the mind for everyday stress at work.**

Vacations do wonders to lift the spirits, put things in perspective, and rejuvenate your goals. It's a time to reflect and explore ideas that you don't have time for when you're working. You can avoid let-downs and vacation disasters if you take more frequent trips instead of one vacation extravaganza. Or take long weekends to give a change of pace.

Vacation Alternatives

Plan a vacation that matches your style. You don't have to spend a lot of money to have fun. Sometimes the more you spend the more you feel obligated to have a good time, and the worse you feel if you don't.

Consider a volunteer vacation. Volunteer vacations are working trips sponsored by organizations that need vacationers to work on their projects. Among the selections are ten-day archeological digs in France, researching whales in the South Pacific, repairing trails in Utah, building schools in Mexico, and teaching swimming to children in Hong Kong. (For more information on volunteer vacations, see the resource section of this book.)

Weekends and Holidays

Well-planned holidays and weekends give you time to reactivate, get the clutter out of your head, and return to your home and job refreshed. Think of days off as a valuable investment in good health. The secret is all in the planning.

VACATIONS, WEEKENDS AND HOLIDAYS (Continued)

PERSONAL-TIME STRATEGIES

Try these personal-time strategies for a successful detachment from routine:

PERSONAL-TIME STRATEGY 1. Escape from your job.

Don't take work home on weekends and holidays. A break from your regular job responsibilities is valuable for good health.

PERSONAL-TIME STRATEGY 2. Split your time.

Divide your holidays and weekends into controllable parts. Plan separate activities for mornings, afternoons, and evenings, making sure to include rest and play between chores.

PERSONAL-TIME STRATEGY 3. Divide errand-running.

Run a few errands at a time and shop during the week, if time permits. Do the remaining errands early on weekends or holidays to free up your schedule for other activities.

PERSONAL-TIME STRATEGY 4. Make notes and organize.

When you are home, write down work ideas and forget them until later. For more focused weekdays, organize the activities for the coming week on Sunday evening or early Monday morning.

WOMEN AND MONEY

VITAL SIGNS—Money
• Of the 3.8 million people with incomes of $75,000 or more, 13% are women.
• Women are more likely than men to rely entirely on Social Security for retirement.

Constant worry about money can jeopardize your physical and emotional health. When your finances are shaky, you feel out of control and stressed.

Take a minute to assess your financial health by taking this five-question quiz:

FINANCIAL HEALTH WORKSHOP FOR WOMEN ONLY

YES   NO

___ ___ Do you pay yourself first?

___ ___ If you are younger than 55, do you have disability insurance?

___ ___ Do you spend a large amount of your monthly income to pay off debts?

___ ___ Are you always aware of the family's finances?

___ ___ Do you have an emergency fund that's just for you?

If you answered yes to all five questions, you have taken some key steps toward a healthy financial future. If you answered no to one or more questions, read on.

WOMEN AND MONEY (Continued)

FINANCIAL HEALTH STRATEGIES

FINANCIAL HEALTH STRATEGY 1. Pay yourself first.

Make yourself top priority and pay yourself first. Begin by listing what you have spent in the last two months. When you know where your money is going, you can identify areas where it is possible to cut back.

Set up a budget that helps you live within your income and save some each month. You may have to work temporarily at a second job to increase your income enough to save. You might even want to send yourself monthly bills to assure that you're putting money away. Put some of your savings in a credit union account, savings account, checking account, or money market fund that easily converts to cash in case of emergency.

FINANCIAL HEALTH STRATEGY 2. Buy supplemental disability insurance.

Disability insurance provides a monthly income if you are disabled and unable to work because of an accident or long-term illness. Many women neglect to plan for these contingencies.

No one is invulnerable to illness or accident, and more people file for disability than you might think. Twenty-eight percent of today's young women and 42% of the men either die or become too disabled to work before age 65.

Don't rely on Social Security disability. Some studies report that up to 80% of all Social Security disability claims are disallowed. Group disability benefits are usually coordinated with worker's compensation, Social Security disability, and pension disability, but the benefits can be discontinued before the employee is ready to go back to work. You have greater protection when you have a supplemental disability insurance policy. (For more important disability insurance information, see the resource section of this book.)

FINANCIAL HEALTH STRATEGY 3. Pay off debts.

The National Foundation for Consumer Credit warns of the signs of excessive debt:

- You cannot pay all your bills each month.
- You obtain a cash advance from one credit card to pay the charges from another.
- You are uneasy about the amount of money you are spending.

The quickest way to solve debt problems is to stop charging until all of your credit cards are paid off. Pay as much as possible as soon as you can to avoid the accruing finance charges on unpaid balances. Once you are debt-free, faithfully use a budget to stay out of debt. If your debt is excessive, seek financial help from a nonprofit consumer-credit counselor.

Make it a priority to borrow only to pay for items that add significantly to your asset base, such as a house, car, or education. To avoid a temptation to spend, limit yourself to two or three credit cards, such as a bank card that covers almost all purchases, a gas credit card, and a charge card from your favorite store. Beware of expensive status credit cards. Low-fee and no-fee bank cards save you money.

Pay attention to payment due dates and interest-free time periods when paying credit card bills. Most credit card companies don't bill the finance charges if you pay the full balance each month.

WOMEN AND MONEY (Continued)

FINANCIAL HEALTH STRATEGY 4. Be financially aware.

Protect yourself and your family by knowing your family's finances, even if you don't pay the monthly bills. Married women are often too busy with their jobs and families to pay attention to financial affairs. They rely on their husbands to budget and pay bills. A sudden crisis or change can be costly if the bill-payer cannot continue to manage the money.

FINANCIAL HEALTH STRATEGY 5. Create a personal emergency fund.

The best insurance a woman can have is an emergency fund that is accessible to her alone. There are no guarantees in life and everyone needs to be prepared for the remotest possibilities.

SINGLE WORKING WOMEN

VITAL SIGNS—Single Working Women

- **The National Academy of Sciences reports that the more an occupation is dominated by women, the less it pays.**
- **A United Nations study found that women do two-thirds of the world's work for only one-tenth of the world's pay.**

The Small Business Administration reports that business start-ups by women have increased dramatically in the past ten years and now make up more than half of all new businesses. But the typical American worker is not a woman who works for a corporation or heads her own company. She is in a service, technical, sales, or administrative occupation.

Office industries are thriving and demand for women workers is healthy, but office pay has fallen behind that of unionized industrial workers. Lack of experience, skills, and education and employment in nonunion, nonindustrial occupations take a toll on women's pay. Some professional women report reaching a "glass ceiling," a level beyond which they are not promoted. On average, women still earn only 64% of what men do.

Women continue to seek pay equity and policy change through such organizations as 9 to 5, National Association of Working Women. Many women are involved in state and national campaigns to improve laws that protect working women on such issues as family and medical leave, retirement benefits, health and safety, and protection for part-time and temporary workers. (Turn to the resource section of this book for addresses of organizations that assist working women.)

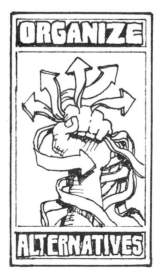

SINGLE WOMEN'S SUCCESS STRATEGIES

It's important how a woman feels about being single. If she feels good about herself, and good about choosing a single life, she'll probably be healthier.

Most single working women flex ''singleness muscles'' to be self-reliant. They pursue five common strategies that make them successful.

SUCCESS STRATEGY 1. Act independently.

Persevering single women take charge of their lives. Their independence is a hard-won, acquired skill, not a genetic blessing.

SUCCESS STRATEGY 2. Take control.

Productive single women minimize the minuses and enhance the pluses. They enroll in night classes, subscribe to new magazines, attend conferences, and read self-improvement books. They are in control.

SUCCESS STRATEGY 3. Expand horizons.

Thriving single women expand their horizons with new friends. They value their friendships and nurture a close-knit community for emotional enrichment.

They expand their interests and drive race cars, study foreign languages, or discover gourmet cooking. They increase their possibilities whenever time and money permit.

SUCCESS STRATEGY 4. Develop connectedness.

Savvy single women put down roots. They link their lives with careers and communities. They connect with the world outside their doors.

SUCCESS STRATEGY 5. Live in the present.

Successful single women make decisions based on what life is, not what it has been or could be. They set goals and work toward them, rather than waiting for ''Prince Charming'' or winning the lottery.

Single women develop confidence and self-esteem when they practice these five strategies. They are good to themselves and they are comfortable with being alone. They see life as a sum of choices and they aren't afraid to make decisions and take some risks.

HARASSMENT

- **It's more likely for a woman than a man to be sexually harassed in the workplace.**
- **Sexual harassment seldom stops unless you make it stop.**

Harassment is a behavior that denigrates, ridicules, or harasses a person because of sex and can include:

- Making derogatory comments about women (or men) in certain jobs

- Sabotaging work

- Ignoring or excluding women or men because of his or her sex

Sexual harassment is also unwelcome behavior of a sexual nature and includes:

- Touching

- Following

- Visuals, including looks or staring

- Gestures

- Comments, innuendoes, or sexual jokes

- Standing close

- Pressuring for dates or sexual acts and making employment decisions or grades conditional upon acceptance or rejection of sexual behavior

Both sexual harassment and sex-based harassment are sexual discrimination and prohibited by federal and state civil rights laws. If you're not sure that you are a victim of sexual harassment, you can call your union, local NOW or 9 to 5 office, or state agency for advice. But always trust your instinct if it tells you that someone's behavior is not okay.

OVERCOMING HARASSMENT

You have several choices for stopping unwelcome sexual behavior. First, use harassment strategy one. If the harassment does not stop, use strategies two to five in order.

HARASSMENT STRATEGY 1. Request a halt.

Tell the harasser to stop. If the person persists, repeat your objections.

HARASSMENT STRATEGY 2. Put it in writing.

If harassment continues, write the person a letter that includes:
- Your perception of the unwelcome behavior
- Where and when the unwelcome actions occurred
- A request that the behavior stop
- A notice that you'll take additional action if the behavior continues
- Your name and the date

Make a copy of the letter and send it by certified mail or give it to the harasser in front of a witness.

HARASSMENT STRATEGY 3. Seek help.

Look for witnesses and others who have been harassed. Many harassers repeat their behavior, and two harassment accusations are harder to ignore than one.

HARASSMENT STRATEGY 4. Talk with your supervisor.

Tell your supervisor about the harassment behavior and ask for help to stop it.

HARASSMENT STRATEGY 5. Follow company procedure.

Use in-company grievance procedures and allow your employer to correct the situation before considering legal action.

HARASSMENT STRATEGY 6. Initiate legal action.

If the harassment continues and your employer does not help you stop it, record everything you have done to stop it. Call the state discrimination agency, the Equal Employment Opportunity Commission, or a legal service agency if you need to take legal action.

MARRIAGE

- **Two-thirds of the dishwashing, child care, paper work, and housecleaning, and 80% of the cooking, laundry, and shopping in the United States are done by women.**
- **When working women were asked about one future duty they wanted assigned to their home robots, the overwhelming response was housecleaning.**

It's not a question anymore of who brings home the bacon. Three-fourths of American women say they expect to work outside their homes most of their adult lives. Women work for the money—and to stay active or enhance their career or personal goals.

Well-documented evidence shows that having a paid job is associated with good physical health. Employed women are healthier than women outside the labor force. Women who feel out of control and overwhelmed by life, whether at home or at a paid job, have the greatest risk of poor health.

Dual Careers

We've come a long way in 200 years when economic life centered around the farm, and spouses did much of their work together. When industry developed, men left home to work and wives stayed home in traditional roles. In the past 50 years, marriage styles shifted and wives joined the work force. The change did not come full circle, however. Most men failed to reclaim their share of the work load at home.

Household-Work Cooperation

According to French actress Marie Daems, all a woman has to do to cure an inferiority complex is go to bed for a day while her husband takes charge of the household.

Wives, whether working or not, continue to do most of the housework. Even though they are not enthusiastic about doing housework, most men say that husbands should help with household chores. More than half agree that the duties should be evenly divided, whether or not the wives have jobs.

Some married working couples share the work load, but they don't expect household chores always to go smoothly. They remember that time-honored saying . . .

Housework can kill you if it's done right!

MARRIAGE STRATEGIES WORKSHOP

The big squeeze in two-job marriages comes from limited time and energy. Use the identification chart to check (✔) valuable ways that you strengthen, or need to strengthen, your marriage as a two-career couple.

STRATEGIES	WE DO THIS	WE SHOULD DO THIS
Don't let careers override the marriage. It's easier to get another job than a good mate.	_____	_____
Make time to do things together. Couples that play and work together, stay together.	_____	_____
Give compliments. Recognize and encourage each others' accomplishments, appearance, and desirable traits.	_____	_____
Exercise together. Sharing a fitness activity enhances communication by giving time to talk and work through problems.	_____	_____
Share financial goals. Set realistic expectations about money and spending.	_____	_____
Develop together intellectually. Conflicts can develop over the years if one partner has grown and the other has slipped backwards.	_____	_____
Be affectionate. Touch, hold hands, and show that you care.	_____	_____
Be friends. Approach your marriage the same way you would a friendship.	_____	_____
Learn how to argue and forgive. Writer Erma Bombeck claims that her marriage has lasted so long because she is a forgiving woman. Long ago she forgave her husband for not being Paul Newman.	_____	_____

HEALTHY PREGNANCY

Working is the healthiest way to spend a pregnancy. Studies indicate that pregnant working women have fewer physical and emotional problems than those who don't work, probably because they keep busy and receive more social support while on the job.

Women who have jobs deliver 50% fewer premature and low-birthweight babies than those who don't. Working women tend to smoke less and seek more medical care, which have positive effects on full-term births and birth weight.

Workplace Pregnancy Policies

Women expecting their first baby remain on the job longer and return to work earlier after giving birth than their counterparts did 25 years ago. In the 1960s, nearly two-thirds of expectant mothers quit their jobs. Now two-thirds receive maternity leave and go back to work.

The Pregnancy Discrimination Act prevents employers from firing women who are pregnant. Pregnancy must be treated as any other disability and expectant mothers can work as long as their doctors say they are able. Some state laws guarantee a specific period for maternity leave and mandate that the job be held open and seniority preserved.

Despite the laws, maternity leave is a crazy-quilt of paid and unpaid work stoppage. Some companies still lack formal pregnancy leave policy; others find it good business to help workers balance their jobs and family responsibilities. Some companies are unaffected by long maternity leaves; others can suffer because a two- or three-month absence can create problems for a workplace with sparse backup resources. Although companies are required to keep the jobs available, sometimes new mothers never return.

HEALTHY PREGNANCY (Continued)

> If you are planning your pregnancy, it could ease your mind to check your employer's maternity-leave policy beforehand. If your employer has no policy, you might be able to implement one or work out a personal plan with your supervisor for your absence.

HEALTHY BABY STRATEGIES

HEALTHY BABY STRATEGY 1. Don't smoke.

Happily, no evidence suggests that even ten or more years of smoking before pregnancy harms a developing fetus. However, continued smoking during pregnancy can cause low birthweight, miscarriage, stillbirth, and premature birth. The effects of cigarette smoking on the baby are directly related to the number of times that the pregnant mother lights up. Babies of women who smoke a pack or more a day during pregnancy suffer a 50% greater death risk.

HEALTHY BABY STRATEGY 2. Avoid alcohol.

Physicians agree that the more alcohol that's consumed during pregnancy, the higher the risk is that the unborn child will suffer physical malformation or mental retardation. Even moderate drinking by an expectant mother during the first two months of pregnancy can affect a baby's intelligence. Children of mothers who drank as little as one or two drinks daily during the first months of pregnancy had lower attention levels and slower reaction times by school age.

The only prevention for alcohol-related problems is for the expectant mother to avoid drinking. Physicians, self-help organizations, and businesses can assist with alcohol cessation programs. (Some organizations that give abstaining assistance are listed in the resource section of this book.)

HEALTHY BABY STRATEGY 3. Beware of harmful substances.

Women who use marijuana, cocaine, heroin, methadone, and other narcotics are more likely to have stillborn or low-birthweight babies. Some prescription drugs such as birth control pills, tranquilizers, and antibiotics are known or thought to cause birth defects or other complications in the baby when taken during pregnancy.

Even aspirin and some other over-the-counter drugs should be avoided during pregnancy. Aspirin and ibuprofen taken during the last three months of pregnancy may cause delivery complications or problems in the unborn child.

Pregnant women or nursing mothers should use hair dyes sparingly because chemical absorption might harm an unborn baby or nursing infant. Touch-ups won't hurt, but expectant or nursing mothers are advised to avoid complete color changes and permanents.

PARENTING

- **Only about 6% of American households rely on the husband as sole provider for a wife and two or more children.**
- **More than half of women with preschool children work outside their homes.**

Rich lifestyles, fascinating men, and glamorous evenings may be the stuff that romance novels are made of, but that's not really what women want, according to *Self Magazine*. Their survey found that most women agreed that the role of a working, married mother is the most satisfying. Only a few women wanted a return to the days of their mothers' stay-at-home generation.

Research shows that households with two working parents have a positive effect on the entire family. Working mothers are economically more secure and feel that they have more control over their lives. Husbands of working wives have less stress knowing that the family financial support is shared by another adult. Usually the better that parents feel about themselves and their financial situations, the better they are as parents.

RALPH MARCON

MAKE ROOM FOR DADDY

Most working mothers today find that assuming full responsibility for household chores and childcare—after putting in a full day at the office—is too exhausting, and they expect their husbands to share the domestic burden. Many men are struggling to adapt to these expectations. More men are sharing household chores, and taking their kids to the dentist.

Although fathers are doing more, they still fall short in child care and domestic duties. Most fathers surveyed said they should be helping more with children, but only 13% said they shared child care equally with their wives.

Fathers may do less for many reasons. Lack of knowledge about child care frightens some men. Others accept their helping roles grudgingly and only because their wives work. For many men, time is limited. The list of fathering responsibilities grows longer, but nothing is taken off the list.

Despite the conflict, men are discovering the advantages of closer family relationships:

- Involved fatherhood gives the satisfaction of a good relationship with children.

- Solid ties with children often strengthen marriages by building partnerships.

- Children benefit by having a close relationship with a male role model.

- Careers are not damaged. One study showed that men who spent a lot of time with their families were as successful in their careers as men who did not.

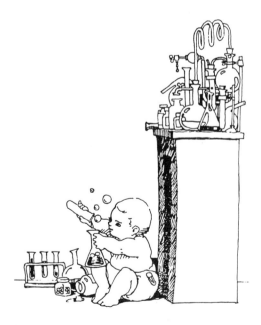

PARENTAL POINTERS

1. *Flexibility*

Grandma was babysitting her five-year-old grandson for a few hours. She phoned her daughter to ask, ''When do you want me to bring Terry home?'' Without hesitation her daughter replied, ''When he's grown up.''

Most parents at some time have felt like they'd gladly trade their child for a sack of potatoes. It's a normal feeling, especially when a colicky baby has cried most of the night or a two-year-old has painted the kitchen with mashed bananas.

Stay loose. Kids' needs are much more variable than the job demands. Parents need to be adaptable.

2. *Commitment*

Commitment is the fundamental element that makes families work. Parents need to commit as much, if not more, effort to their families as they do to their careers. Commitment to the family is the first priority in strong families.

3. *Exercise*

Children and adolescents are becoming less physically fit and score lower on endurance, strength, and flexibility tests. Parents can encourage physical activity by participating with their kids in activities like biking, skiing, or hiking. Physically active children are more likely to have better strength, flexibility, coordination, physical health, motor development, and regular sleeping patterns.

THE PARENT TRACK

Having a family takes more energy, money, and time than anyone ever suspects. A tiny, six-pound baby demands—usually with great volume—attention. And you don't get weekends and holidays off when you're a parent. Parenting is a full-time job.

Time is the working parent's scarcest commodity. In a recent survey, almost half of working parents said that they do not spend enough time with their families. Ironically, half of the children of working mothers indicated, in a different study, that they wished their mothers could spend more time with them.

Children need parental attention most during their first ten years. And family time does not just happen; it is planned.

MAKING TIME COUNT STRATEGIES

TIME STRATEGY 1. Talk with your kids.

Ask them questions. Encourage conversation.

TIME STRATEGY 2. Be there for them.

Focus all your attention on your children, not half on television or another distraction. Keep eye contact. Small amounts of attention when they need it are worth a lot.

TIME STRATEGY 3. Be positive.

Attitudes are learned. Kids love to be told, ''You did a good job.'' A pat on the back is a powerful motivator.

TIME STRATEGY 4. Spend leisurely time with your children.

Read them a story, take a walk, or go to the zoo. Hours spent with children become cherished memories.

TIME STRATEGY 5. Promote mealtime togetherness.

Make mealtime conversations so vital and stimulating that your family will want to linger at the table. Establish specific mealtimes. Unplug the phone. Discuss healthy foods.

TIME STRATEGY 6. Be affectionate.

Give lots of hugs.

SINGLE PARENTS

VITAL SIGNS—Single Parents

- **Experiencing first-hand successes, mistakes, and emotional ups and downs brings a special closeness between single parents and children.**
- **Approximately one family in six is headed by a single woman.**

Families are increasingly headed by single parents. It does not take much arithmetic to suggest that when one person has to do all the caring and work that is usually shared by two people, more time and energy are required.

While it's important not to minimize the difficulties of being a single parent, many women see positive sides to single parenting. One primary advantage is the time spent together building a closer relationship with the child. Often it's not the child-oriented activity like going to the circus, but cooking meals or folding laundry that translates into time together. Chore-time can provide valuable talk-time with children and a chance for them to learn to care for themselves, survive, and thrive.

SINGLE PARENT STRATEGIES

Use these useful parenting strategies to minimize time and energy demands.

SINGLE PARENT STRATEGY 1. Seek others who can help.

Coordinate a skills exchange and share baby-sitting with friends. Carpool for children's activities whenever possible.

SINGLE PARENT STRATEGY 2. Have a realistic outlook.

Be practical about expectations. You can't do it all.

SINGLE PARENT STRATEGY 3. Allow enough time.

You'll be a better parent when you give yourself the time and opportunity to feel good about yourself.

AGING PARENTS

- **Women spend an average of 17 years caring for children and 18 years caring for parents.**
- **Only 5% of Americans older than 65 live in nursing homes.**

Actress Ruth Gordon claimed that her most successful achievement after reaching age 65 was becoming 66. And after that, it was getting to be 67, 68, and on into her 80s. Like many older people, she approached aging as a challenge and continued to be productive into later life.

People today are living longer than ever. Modern medicine accounts for many of those added years, but lifestyle changes also have helped. Today's aging population is exercising more, eating more sensibly, smoking and drinking less, and approaching retirement age with a resolve to stay active.

Resolve can break down when illness or other serious problems strike. And when difficulty arises, women in the middle generation are often thrust into caregiving roles that significantly alter their lives.

The Sandwich Generation

It's late in the afternoon and the school coach calls Laura at work. Her son hurt his leg during practice and needs to see his doctor. Could she leave work early and pick him up?

Laura had promised to take her ailing mother grocery shopping after work. And after dinner, she and her husband had planned to see their daughter's new apartment.

Laura is a classic member of the "sandwich generation" who must cope with an aging parent and also care for her children, even after they are grown.

For the first time in history, the average American family has more parents than children. As women delay having children and adults live longer, more women find themselves caring for both children and an aging parent. Since three of every four women are the primary caregivers, the parent requiring care may be an in-law.

As medicine advances, parents can conceivably be in their children's care for 20 or 25 years. For the woman caregiver, the toll on her immediate family and her job can be disastrous.

CAREGIVING STRATEGIES ⟹

CAREGIVING STRATEGIES

If you are in the sandwich generation and an aging parent needs extra help, consider these six strategies to minimize your time demands and help ease potential caregiving problems:

CAREGIVING STRATEGY 1. Don't neglect your own family.

Be careful not to neglect your family to care for a parent. Sometimes immediate family needs are overlooked and family members take a back seat. This only compounds the problem.

CAREGIVING STRATEGY 2. Evaluate the time spent with your parent.

If you feel compelled to visit frequently or feel guilty if you don't, your visits are probably not pleasant for you or your parent. A once-a-week visit that is less rushed might be better than visits several times a week.

CAREGIVING STRATEGY 3. Work as a family unit.

Make caring for a parent a family affair. Ask family members for help and make sure they understand why their help is necessary.

CAREGIVING STRATEGY 4. Join a support group.

Consider joining a short-term caregivers support group if your parent is manipulative or unreasonable about demanding time with you. Support groups offer valuable ideas and help to relieve stress.

CAREGIVING STRATEGY 5. Locate additional services.

Contact your local or state agency on aging to find out what programs are offered. You'll be surprised at the number of support services that are usually available.

CAREGIVING STRATEGY 6. Seek outside help.

Use a third party as a buffer when the relationship with your parent is difficult. A mutual friend, doctor, or social worker without emotional ties might communicate more easily with your parent.

WOMEN'S FRIENDSHIPS AND HEALTH

VITAL SIGNS—Friendship

- **Studies show that people who have friends are healthier and live longer.**
- **Most women continue to make friends throughout their lives while men lose old friends and do not replace them.**

The importance of friendship to health and well-being has surfaced in the past decade and even government has gotten into the act. The California Department of Health sponsors radio and television public service announcements promoting the physical and mental health value of friendship. ''Make a friend,'' their advertisements coax. ''Friends can be good medicine.''

Sharing the ups and downs of life and having someone to confide in lessens stress and contributes to wellness. People without friends suffer higher risks of cancer, hospitalizations, and premature death than those with a network of friends.

Men's and Women's Friendships: The Differences

At every stage in life, women have more friends than men. Women's friendships often center on shared personal feelings, emotional support, and nurturing. Men share activities and tend to ''do'' rather than ''be'' in their friendships.

Women use the term ''friend'' more selectively than men. Men are likely to identify friends as members of their ball team, co-workers, or neighbors, even if they don't know them well. To some men, friends are people they don't dislike.

Most women spend more time than men nurturing friendships because they value the relationships so highly. Women generally think of friends as a mutual support to strengthen their emotional lives. Men often do not recognize friends as a support system and do not rely on them.

WORKPLACE FRIENDSHIPS

Work can be the best place to make friends. Just as women used to talk across the back fence, today's women often make friends and talk with others who share the next office.

Friends can make bad jobs better. Friendship at the workplace can make a day bearable and contribute to better mental health.

Employees who are happy together are more efficient and productive. When co-workers talk to each other and let off steam, companies benefit with higher morale, fewer medical expenses, and less absenteeism.

Hours together, shared space, and job understanding contribute to workplace friendships. Working together for a long time fosters closeness that is a natural means for making friends. In many cases, work relationships become extended families for co-workers.

FRIENDSHIP STRATEGIES

It is a mistake to choose only friends who act and think the same as you do. When friends are all the same there is not room to grow in the friendship.

FRIENDSHIP STRATEGY 1. Develop friends of different ages.

The most common friendships are among people the same age. You'll enrich your life when you make friends who are both younger and older than you. Become a special friend to a child in your block. Benefit from the association and experience of an elderly person.

FRIENDSHIP STRATEGY 2. Stay in touch with old friends.

Send a letter or quick postcard, pick up the phone, or make an effort to visit longtime friends. When true friends meet each other, uneasy feelings from years of separation can disappear after five minutes of talk.

FRIENDSHIP STRATEGY 3. Choose your friends carefully.

It's much more fun to be around friends who laugh and see the bright side of the world.

In a good friendship, both people are energized by the relationship. If friends make you feel drained and exhausted, you need to examine the time and energy that you put into the friendship. Stop seeing a person if the relationship is no longer mutually supportive and interesting. It's better to cultivate and nurture fewer friendships than many superficial acquaintances.

GET-TOGETHER STRATEGIES

If you haven't had time to see friends, consider these timesaving strategies to get your friends together. Pay your kids or the neighbor's children to help serve and clean up.

GET-TOGETHER STRATEGY 1. Sunday brunch.

Brunch is an easy way to have several friends in at once. Prepare a fast and simple menu on Saturday and use Sunday afternoon to clean up.

GET-TOGETHER STRATEGY 2. Make your own sundaes.

Put out healthy fresh fruit toppings and invite friends to enjoy after-dinner, low-fat yogurt sundaes.

GET-TOGETHER STRATEGY 3. Potluck dinner.

You provide the clean house and beverages while each friend contributes one food item to a potluck gathering.

GET-TOGETHER STRATEGY 4. Summertime picnic.

Invite friends over to barbecue hot dogs or hamburgers. Add a pot of beans, a fresh vegetable tray, and other healthy, easy-to-fix foods.

GET-TOGETHER STRATEGY 5. Simple winter fare.

Fix soup or chili and serve with a tossed salad, bread, coffee, and bars.

GET-TOGETHER STRATEGY 6. Formal parties.

If you feel ambitious and want to catch up on entertaining many friends, have back-to-back open house parties (1:00 to 3:00 p.m. and 4:00 to 6:00 p.m.), or open house gatherings two days in a row. The house is picked up, dishes and silverware are out, and you can use the same menu for both events.

GET-TOGETHER STRATEGY 7. Walk with a friend.

You'll get some exercise and a chance to catch up at the same time.

GET-TOGETHER STRATEGY 8. Take your kids to the park with a friend.

Your children can play while you sit and talk.

GET-TOGETHER STRATEGY 9. Become patrons of the arts or sports enthusiasts.

Buy season tickets with a friend to the local theater, symphony, or sports events. Then go for dinner before or a drink afterward.

GET-TOGETHER STRATEGY 10. Volunteer together.

Many charitable organizations rely on volunteer members. Join with a friend or group of friends to lick envelopes or cook and serve meals. You'll be serving your community and staying in touch at the same time.

GET-TOGETHER STRATEGY 11. Run errands together.

Everybody has to do laundry or grocery shopping. Set aside your Saturday morning to do chores with a friend.

S E C T I O N

II

Wellness Strategies

Imagine...

Awakening each morning and feeling so energized that you can't wait to begin the day.

Imagine...

365 days each year of continuous good health. You can do it!

Begin by focusing on the eight wellness strategies that are described on the following pages. Each strategy is an action plan designed to help you take charge of your health and make healthy lifestyle choices. The strategies are all interrelated like they are in the wellness wheel. One won't work successfully without the others.

Make this a turning point in your life and choose wellness. It's a winning decision that you won't regret!

SLEEP, WONDERFUL SLEEP

VITAL SIGNS—Sleep

- Sleep experts find that most of us sleep 60–90 minutes less each night than we should, and the effects of sleep-loss are cumulative.
- Keep the bedroom at 60–65°F for ideal slumber. Physical activity increases when it's above 70°. Dreams will awaken you when the temperature is below 54°.

We spend 24½ years of our lives sleeping, but most of us don't get enough sleep. One bad night's sleep can make you less efficient on mental tasks. Sleep-loss lowers energy levels and causes attention lapses. It's not as easy to enjoy a joke or feel pleasure if you haven't had enough sleep.

Sleep experts say that most people try to make up for insufficient sleep by sleeping more on weekends. In cases of constant sleep loss, a weekend of ten-hour nights is not sufficient.

Staying awake to accomplish more usually backfires, too. Lack of sleep severely limits productivity. You will be more creative and focused when you have adequate sleep, even though your waking hours are fewer.

Some women need to sleep only a few hours a night while others require as much as ten hours or more per night. The best rule for sleep fitness is to go to bed at approximately the same time each night and rise at the same time each morning. You are shortening your natural sleep pattern if you need an alarm clock to wake up.

REASONS WHY WE DON'T SLEEP

Lack of exercise

You may not be getting sufficient exercise if you sleep enough and still feel groggy in the morning. Exercise makes the body use oxygen more efficiently. You sleep better and awaken more refreshed.

Reaction to drugs

The leading fatigue-causing medications are antibiotics, diuretics, pain-relievers, and antihistamines. Consuming alcohol and sleeping pills also disrupts sleep. Alcohol consumption prevents deep sleep and pills don't wear off entirely until the next day.

Lack of natural light

The hormone melatonin, which regulates the sleep cycle, is disrupted by the lack of sunlight. Tinted windshields, artificial office light, and sunglasses may interfere with the natural light we need to help us sleep.

Worrying about sleeplessness

Staying awake one night can cause more mental than physical harm. We worry that our performance will be impaired and we won't be able to fall asleep the next night. Relax! The body usually adjusts to lost sleep by pumping more adrenalin into the system.

Physical disorders

Diseases can interrupt the body's delicate wake-sleep mechanism because the body's metabolism is altered when it fights infection. That's why a thorough physical examination is an important first step in treating sleeplessness.

SLEEP STRATEGIES

TAKE A WARM BATH.

People who take baths before retiring show deeper-sleep brainwave activity. Bubble baths are even better because the suds help keep the water warm.

KEEP PHYSICALLY ACTIVE.

Stay active after a sleepless night. Activity oxygenates your body, makes you feel less tired, and promotes better sleep the next night.

COUNT SHEEP.

Any creative counting (odd/even numbers, backwards, in sequences) may be helpful in falling asleep. Counting prevents disturbing thoughts from entering and centers on repetitive, senseless patterns that may make you sleepy.

AVOID STRESSFUL SITUATIONS.

Relax with reading, quiet music, or television before bedtime.

DRINK WARM MILK.

Take Grandma's advice and drink warm milk at bedtime. Avoid beverages that contain caffeine such as chocolate, colas, tea, and coffee.

DON'T GO TO BED UNTIL YOU'RE SLEEPY.

When you don't feel sleepy, get out of bed and do something that interests you until you feel ready for bed. Or try telling yourself that it's time to sleep, you're ready to relax, you want to sleep, and you *are* going to sleep!

READ A COMPLEX OR BORING BOOK.

If you keep a book on your bedstand that you "should read" such as a serious treatment of history, chances are good you won't last more than a few pages.

VIM, VIGOR, AND VITAL EXERCISE

> **VITAL SIGNS—Exercise**
>
> - Each stair that you climb adds four seconds to your life.
> - A Harvard study determined that exercising women are less likely to develop breast and reproductive system cancer than non-exercising women.

Your body is meant to move. Useful exercise doesn't have to be strenuous. Vigorous exercise can injure women who aren't usually active.

Routine physical activity can help protect your body. Home chores like washing windows and weeding, carrying the baby, and climbing stairs help maintain and tone the body. Even moderate exercise helps prevent disabling ailments such as obesity, diabetes, depression, osteoporosis, heart disease, and high blood pressure.

Benefits from physical exercise make you feel better about yourself. When you exercise you:

- Increase flexibility
- Prevent disease
- Gain energy
- Lower blood pressure
- Feel more joy
- Improve heart rate
- Decrease depression
- Increase work capacity
- Strengthen muscles
- Feel accomplishment

CALORIE BURNING WORKSHOP

Even if you think you are a couch potato, you might be surprised at the amount of activity and exercise that you get. Have some fun and match the activities and the calories that are burned with each activity.

Answers: A. (80–120 calories)
B. (121–310 calories)
C. (311–480 calories)
D. (481–625 calories)

ACTIVITIES	CALORIES BURNED BY 150-POUND ADULT
Weeding garden	1. _____
Standing quietly	2. _____
Walking quickly (4 mph)	3. _____
Shopping	4. _____
Running (7 mph)	5. _____
Cleaning house	6. _____
Cycling (9 mph)	7. _____
Scrubbing floors	8. _____
Aerobic dancing	9. _____
Office work	10. _____

ANSWERS: (1.C) (2.A) (3.C) (4.B) (5.D) (6.B) (7.C) (8.C) (9.D) (10.B)

WHEN AND WHERE TO EXERCISE

Morning exercises are a good way to work out regularly. As the day progresses, it's easier not to exercise. When foul weather has you trapped indoors, walk in an airport terminal or shopping mall. Many people do it. You might meet an interesting "walking partner."

Exercising regularly is more important than intensity. Light exertion for 30–70 minutes every day (gardening, bowling, home repairs) gives you the same health benefits as strenuous exercise three times a week.

Divide exercise sessions to conquer time constraints. Ten-minute sessions three times a day are as effective as 30-minute sessions once a day.

EXERCISE STRATEGIES

Assess your health and limitations before beginning an exercise program. Get a medical checkup if you have not exercised recently. Consider these six exercise strategies before you begin:

EXERCISE STRATEGY 1. Choose a fun exercise program.

You won't continue to exercise if you don't enjoy it.

EXERCISE STRATEGY 2. Set exercise goals.

Decide on specific goals like swimming five laps, three times weekly this month and seven laps, three times weekly next month. Review your progress each month for a feeling of accomplishment.

EXERCISE STRATEGY 3. Reward yourself.

A new piece of clothing, a long hot bath, or a movie can do wonders to reinforce your goals.

EXERCISE STRATEGY 4. Go slowly.

Start at a level you can handle. Exercise injuries result from impatience, uncurbed optimism, and misunderstanding about the body's adaptation to sudden exercise.

EXERCISE STRATEGY 5. Try an occasional change.

A different time, activity, or program helps to avoid monotony.

EXERCISE STRATEGY 6. Take a break.

Intermittent time off can revitalize waning enthusiasm.

EATING RIGHT

***V**ITAL SIGNS—Food*

- **The human body is an amazing machine at turning food into fuel. If our bodies used gasoline instead of food, our fuel efficiency would be more than 900 miles per gallon.**
- **An adult stomach has 35 million digestive glands with stomach acid so powerful that it can dissolve razor blades in less than a week. The stomach must produce a new lining every three days to avoid digesting itself.**

Our bodies have complex nutritional requirements and no two women have the same needs. We each process differently the 40 nutrients we need for good health. That's why sodium or sugar can be relatively harmless for some women and lethal for others.

Iron Watch

Women must be aware of differences that cause nutritional deficiencies. Iron deficiency interferes with the body's ability to adjust to low temperatures and will sometimes occur because of women's monthly blood loss. Women who frequently feel cold should have their iron levels tested.

Tea and coffee inhibit a woman's ability to absorb iron. You absorb more iron from the food you eat if you don't drink coffee or tea with meals.

EATING STRATEGIES

Women eat more often in a day than they did a decade ago, yet most American women fail to meet all their nutritional requirements.

To get the most out of your meals, try these three eating strategies.

EATING STRATEGY 1. Start with fruit.

Begin your day with juice or a fruit cup. The vitamin C in the fruit aids digestion. When fruit is followed with an iron-rich food like lean ham, the body absorbs twice the iron.

EATING STRATEGY 2. Eat the same amount.

You improve your job performance when you eat the same amount each day. You are less energetic and less able to concentrate and control your weight when you eat small amounts of food one day and large amounts the next.

EATING STRATEGY 3. Don't miss lunch.

Skipping lunch hinders alertness by causing afternoon fatigue. A light 300-calorie lunch provides enough energy to keep you attentive throughout the day. Choose proteins such as a small serving of meat, poultry, seafood, low-fat yogurt, or low-fat cheese to increase afternoon concentration.

BATTLE OF THE BULGE

VITAL SIGNS—*Weight*

- **The typical adult must eat 39 potatoes to gain one pound.**
- **Researchers at Stanford Medical Center say that women can calculate their ideal weight by multiplying 3.5 by their height in inches and subtracting 108.**

Not all calories count the same. The amounts of food that you eat are not as important as the kind of calories that you consume. Your body is much more efficient at converting and storing fats than carbohydrates like breads, potatoes, and beans.

You burn only 3% of the calories when your body stores high-fat foods. You burn 23% of the calories when your body stores carbohydrates. The result is that you may gain weight twice as quickly when you eat the same number of calories in fatty foods as in carbohydrates.

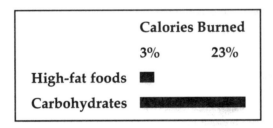

	Calories Burned	
	3%	23%
High-fat foods	■	
Carbohydrates	████████████	

By cutting dietary fat, you decrease your risk of heart disease, the number one killer of women. Another bonus to low-fat eating is that women report fewer menstrual symptoms and less bloating than women on unrestricted diets.

WEIGHT CONTROL STRATEGIES

The first weight a woman loses when dieting is water, not fat. Continual dieting signals the brain to slow metabolism so that calories are burned more slowly. When you lose weight, you need fewer calories to maintain the lower weight.

WEIGHT CONTROL STRATEGY 1. Add fiber.

You can lose weight by adding more fiber to your diet. An increase in the amount of natural fiber helps weight loss in two ways:

- Fiber makes you feel full without burdening you with extra calories.
- Fiber is difficult to digest—so it passes rapidly through the body, taking unneeded calories with it.

Diet Alert

Obesity and crash diets can cause gallstones. Women who are overweight by as few as 15 to 20 pounds are twice as likely to develop gallstones as slim women. Women who try to lose weight by fasting or drastically reducing calories have a high risk of developing gallstones.

WEIGHT CONTROL STRATEGY 2. Increase activity.

You can burn an extra 400–800 calories in a 24-hour period by increasing spontaneous physical activities. Park your car at the farthest point in the parking lot and walk a little farther than usual. Take the stairs instead of the elevator. Even fidgeting in your chair helps burn extra calories.

STORM CLOUDS OF SMOKE

- **You can save enough money to operate a car by not smoking. When you smoke two packs a day you spend approximately the same amount that you spend on the annual upkeep of an automobile.**
- **80–90% of ex-smokers have quit on their own through will-power and determination.**

Ponder These Pluses

Stopping smoking is rarely an event. It's a process. Women may try to quit several times before they succeed, but shortly after a smoker quits, coughs disappear. A nonsmoker feels better, has more energy, and enjoys the self-confidence that comes when taking control of a demanding habit.

Your skin benefits when you kick the tobacco habit. Smoking reduces the blood circulation to the skin resulting in deep wrinkles around the eyes and lips. That yellow-gray skin pallor changes to a healthy, rosy color when smoking does not restrict the skin's blood supply.

Career development is enhanced for nonsmokers. A recent survey found that when candidates were equally qualified, nonsmokers were hired by a ratio of 15 to one over smokers.

It's never too late to quit smoking. Women at risk for heart disease who quit smoking reduced their disease risk regardless of age.

The Bad News Gets Worse
- One in every six deaths in the United States is related to smoking.
- Lung cancer now exceeds breast cancer as the number one cause of cancer death in women.
- Smoking is a major contributor to the third leading cause of death in the United States—strokes.
- Smoking is the most preventable cause of death—yet people continue to smoke.

WHY DO YOU SMOKE?

Here are some statements made by people to describe what they get out of smoking cigarettes. How often do you feel this way when smoking? Circle one number for each statement. Answer every question.

	always	frequently	occasionally	seldom	never
A. I smoke cigarettes to keep myself from slowing down.	5	4	3	2	1
B. Handling a cigarette is part of the enjoyment of smoking it.	5	4	3	2	1
C. Smoking cigarettes is pleasant and relaxing.	5	4	3	2	1
D. I light up a cigarette when I feel angry about something.	5	4	3	2	1
E. When I run out of cigarettes I find it almost unbearable until I can get them.	5	4	3	2	1
F. I smoke cigarettes automatically without even being aware of it.	5	4	3	2	1
G. I smoke cigarettes to stimulate me, to perk myself up.	5	4	3	2	1
H. Part of the enjoyment of smoking a cigarette comes from the steps I take to light up.	5	4	3	2	1
I. I find cigarettes pleasurable.	5	4	3	2	1
J. When I feel uncomfortable or upset about something, I light up a cigarette.	5	4	3	2	1
K. I am very much aware of when I am not smoking a cigarette.	5	4	3	2	1
L. I light up a cigarette without realizing I still have one burning in the ashtray.	5	4	3	2	1
M. I smoke cigarettes to give me a ''lift.''	5	4	3	2	1
N. When I smoke a cigarette, part of the enjoyment is watching the smoke as I exhale it.	5	4	3	2	1
O. I want a cigarette most when I am comfortable and relaxed.	5	4	3	2	1
P. When I feel ''blue'' or want to take my mind off cares and worries, I smoke cigarettes.	5	4	3	2	1
Q. I get a real gnawing hunger for a cigarette when I haven't smoked for a while.	5	4	3	2	1
R. I've found a cigarette in my mouth and didn't remember putting it there.	5	4	3	2	1

Reprinted with permission from the National Cancer Institute.

HOW TO SCORE

1. Enter the number you have circled for each question in the spaces below, putting the number you circled for question A over line A, for question B over line B, etc.

2. Add the three scores on each line to get your totals. For example, the sum of your scores over lines A, G, and M gives you your score on stimulation—lines B, H, and N give the score on handling.

Totals

_____ +	_____ +	_____ =	_____	
A	G	M	Stimulation	
_____ +	_____ +	_____ =	_____	
B	H	N	Handling	
_____ +	_____ +	_____ =	_____	
C	I	O	Pleasurable Relaxation	
_____ +	_____ +	_____ =	_____	
D	J	P	Crutch: Tension Reduction	
_____ +	_____ +	_____ =	_____	
E	K	Q	Craving: Psychological Addiction	
_____ +	_____ +	_____ =	_____	
F	L	R	Habit	

The six factors measured by this test describe different ways of experiencing or managing certain kinds of feelings. Three of these feeling-states represent the positive feelings people get from smoking: increased energy or stimulation; the satisfaction of handling or manipulating things; and the enhancing of pleasurable feelings accompanying a state of well-being. The fourth is the decreasing of negative feelings by reducing tension, anxiety, anger, shame, etc. The fifth is a complex pattern of increasing and decreasing ''craving'' for a cigarette, representing a psychological addiction to smoking. The sixth is habit smoking, which takes place in an absence of feeling—purely automatic smoking.

Scores can vary from 3 to 15. A score of 11 or above on any factor indicates that this factor is an important source of satisfaction for you. The higher your score (15 is the highest), the more important the factor is in your smoking and the more useful the discussion of that factor can be in your efforts to quit.

50

SMOKING WORKSHOP

SUMMARY

50

If you do not score high on any of the six factors, chances are that you do not smoke very much or have not been smoking for very many years. If so, giving up smoking and staying off should be easy.

If you score high in several categories, you apparently get several kinds of satisfaction from smoking and will have to find several solutions. Certain combinations of scores may indicate that giving up smoking will be especially difficult. Those who score high on both factors **four** and **five**, reduction of negative feelings and craving, may have a particularly hard time in going off smoking and in staying off. However, it can be done; many smokers represented by this combination have been able to quit.

Others who score high on factors **one** and **five** may find it useful to change their smoking patterns and cut down at the same time. They can try to smoke fewer cigarettes, smoke them only half-way down, use low-tar/nicotine cigarettes, and inhale less often and less deeply. After several months of this temporary solution, these smokers may find it easier to stop completely.

You must make two decisions: (1) whether to try to do without the satisfactions you get from smoking or find an appropriate, less hazardous substitute, and (2) whether to cut out cigarettes all at once or taper off.

Your scores should guide you in making these decisions.

THAT KEYED-UP FEELING

VITAL SIGNS—Stress

- **Stress inhibits the body's immune system and lessens a woman's ability to fight infection and disease. Saliva tests taken from students during final exams showed decreased levels of infection-fighting antibodies compared with samples taken two weeks after the exams.**
- **Studies at the University of Wisconsin show that reduced stress levels last only 20 minutes after 40 minutes of rest but last 3 hours after the same amount of exercise.**

Stress is an adrenal reaction or response to something. It is caused by conflict: we think we should be doing more than we are, or we are worried about what our children are doing when we're at work, or we are frightened that our salaries might not cover our bills.

Conflict in work relationships is a big cause of stress for working women. Interactions with people you hardly know create significantly more stress than conflicts with caring family members or friends. Sales clerks, customer service representatives, and other service professionals who have no personal relationship with the people they serve are the most prone to psychological stress. People who have little or no power to affect their working conditions also experience stress.

Even when we know fellow workers, office problems may be more stressful than domestic problems. Office relationships often don't have the level of affection or intimacy that allows women to discuss problems or vent anger.

Stress affects the body in many ways. Headaches, neck and shoulder tension, anxiety, edginess, and fatigue are stress symptoms. Stress can also be hidden until more serious illnesses, such as hypertension, develop.

BURN-OUT WORKSHOP

It takes less time to become stressed than to recover from stress-induced illness. Many stress-related illnesses, such as strokes and heart attacks, can be killers. Evaluate how close you are to dangerous levels of stress by taking the burn-out quiz from *The Book of Inside Information* published by Bottom Line.

Scoring: 10 = strong affirmative (SA)
7 = affirmative (A)
3 = negative (N)
0 = strong negative (SN)

SA	A	N	SN	
____	____	____	____	Are you fatigued throughout the day?
____	____	____	____	Do you speak up less often in business (work) meetings than you used to?
____	____	____	____	Are you forgetting things more frequently?
____	____	____	____	Are you tired after a good night's sleep?
____	____	____	____	Does your mind always seem in full gear?
____	____	____	____	Do you seem further behind at the end of the day?
____	____	____	____	Are you less patient with others?
____	____	____	____	Do you spend less time on hobbies?
____	____	____	____	Are accomplishments seldom pleasing to you?
____	____	____	____	Do you constantly operate at full speed during waking hours?

EVALUATION:

0-15 points indicates you are either totally inactive or have your act together, 16-50 shows you are unlikely to suffer from burn-out, 51-80 indicates that burn-out could be close, 86-100 means you are a walking time bomb.

STRESS-BUSTING STRATEGIES

If you are on the high end of the stress scale, consider these eight stress-busters.

STRESS-BUSTING STRATEGY 1. Exercise.

Exercise is one of the best ways to boost immunity and reduce stress. An aerobically conditioned heart beats slower in stressful situations and you remain more calm and in control.

STRESS-BUSTING STRATEGY 2. Slow down.

Assess your activities. Engaging in too many activities can be overwhelming and stressful. Gradually eliminate nonfulfilling obligations and take time to slow down.

STRESS-BUSTING STRATEGY 3. Smile.

A single smile can help you handle stress. Your body associates pleasant feelings with smiling and responds accordingly, even when you don't have anything to smile about.

STRESS-BUSTING STRATEGY 4. Relax.

Close your eyes, breathe rhythmically, and blot out distractions for 10–15 minutes each day to reduce stress. Or use a progressive relaxation technique by lying on a firm surface, breathing deeply, and gradually tensing your muscles from head to toe for 30 seconds. Repeat three times.

STRESS-BUSTING STRATEGY 5. Smell some food.

Your nose can help you reduce stress. Smelling food lowers stress and psychologists theorize that food odors trigger pleasant memories that cause the body to relax. Even thoughts of food can be relaxing.

The nose is a wondrous mechanism. Nostrils switch off every three or four hours so that one closes down and rests while the other is smelling and breathing.

Put a nostril to work, relax, and reduce stress with some delicious, low-calorie smells!

STRESS-BUSTING STRATEGIES (Continued)

STRESS-BUSTING STRATEGY 6. Eat right.

Most of us don't think of good nutrition as a stress-reducer, but we can compound stress with poor eating and drinking habits. Sugar affects how you feel. Caffeine is a stimulant and makes things worse when you are stressed. Alcohol is a depressant and slows some brain functions.

Foods that are high in vitamin B and calcium are stress-fighters. When you are stressed, eat milk products that contain calcium and foods such as meats, tuna, and beans that are high in vitamin B.

STRESS-BUSTING STRATEGY 7. Talk to yourself.

We all have self-talks that are needlessly negative. Be positive and discipline yourself not to overreact. Take control of your emotions and you'll be less stressed.

Put an "Enjoy Life" reminder on your desk or table.

ENJOY LIFE—THIS IS NOT A DRESS REHEARSAL!

STRESS-BUSTING STRATEGY 8. Identify your values.

You feel more stressed when you run on someone else's fast track, not your own. Pretend you only have a short time to live. Make three lists.

> List A • Things I have to do.
>
> List B • Things I want to do.
>
> List C • Things I don't have to do or don't want to do.

For the rest of your life, forget about doing everything on list three. Your values will be prioritized and you'll be less stressed.

SEEK SOLITUDE

VITAL SIGNS—Solitude

- **Women assume caregiving roles more often than men and need time alone and away from the people they care for.**
- *"One hour of thoughtful solitude may nerve the heart for days of conflict"...Percival*

The emotional needs of working women often are not met when they don't have time to be alone. Many women spend their days in constant motion, attending meetings, doing household tasks, or pacing when on the phone. They are caught up in doing and often don't take solitary time to think, deliberate, or reflect.

Women often feel less comfortable than men going off to spend time by themselves. They attempt to solve problems by talking about their feelings. Or they try to get away by retreating with others, and that sometimes worsens the problem.

Women need introspection to know what their work goals are before they can be effective employees. When they take time to know themselves and set priorities, they don't get overly involved in job details and lose track of who they are.

Most marriage relationships are strengthened when spouses spend time apart. Married partners are less irritable, critical, and feel less smothered when they give each other the chance to enjoy some solitude.

SOLITUDE STRATEGIES

SOLITUDE STRATEGY 1. Take time for solitude.

Sit down by yourself for 30 minutes each day. Read, plan, relax, write, think, dream, stretch, meditate, or reminisce.

SOLITUDE STRATEGY 2. Discuss solitude.

Talk about the benefits of solitude and your desire to be alone so that others don't misinterpret your needs and feel rejected.

S E C T I O N

III

Know Your Body

You aren't guaranteed a disease- or injury-free life, but the care you give your body today will be reflected in the way you feel and look 20 years from now. Be aware of disease and other factors that affect your health. The more you know about yourself and wellness, the more likely you are to make informed decisions about your health.

THE BODY'S TIMECLOCK

> ### *VITAL SIGNS—Body's Timeclock*
>
> - **More than 100 internal bodily functions such as blood pressure, temperature, and hormone levels rise and fall at different times during the day.**
> - **Long-term memory is more accurate in the afternoon and short-term memory is 15% more efficient in the morning.**

Whether you remember a person's name or an address may depend on the time of day that you first heard them. Circadian rhythms, the 24-hour cycles that regulate most bodily functions, often affect the things you remember, say, and do.

Circadian rhythms also influence alertness, emotions, and energy levels. You can feel on top of the world at 9:00 a.m. and in the dregs by 3:00 p.m. Your body isn't being tricky, it's simply making necessary adjustments.

The body gears up in the morning. Energy, alertness, and enthusiasm peak in mid- or late-morning and decrease in early afternoon. Re-energizing often happens by mid-afternoon only to taper off again after 4:00 p.m.

PERSONAL CYCLE LOG WORKSHOP

Pay attention to your body's rhythms when you plan your daily activities. Use the personal cycle log for a week to determine when your energy level is the highest.

TIME	ACTIVITY Type of task	ENERGY LEVEL Low, Moderate, High
8:00–9:00 a.m.	_____	_____
9:00–10:00 a.m.	_____	_____
10:00–11:00 a.m.	_____	_____
11:00–12:00 p.m.	_____	_____
12:00–1:00 p.m.	_____	_____
1:00–2:00 p.m.	_____	_____
2:00–3:00 p.m.	_____	_____
3:00–4:00 p.m.	_____	_____
4:00–5:00 p.m.	_____	_____

Take advantage of your body's timeclock. Once you have charted your personal cycles, you can accomplish more by scheduling more important or difficult tasks when your energy and productivity levels are the highest.

#1 KILLER OF WOMEN

> ### *VITAL SIGNS—Heart Disease*
>
> - **One in nine women aged 45–64 has heart disease. This ratio increases to one in three women after age 65.**
> - **More women die of heart disease than of all forms of cancer combined.**

MYTH: Women can relax about heart attacks because heart disease usually strikes middle-aged men.

TRUTH: Heart disease is the number one killer of women. However, lifestyle changes can help prevent heart disease.

RISK FACTORS THAT YOU CAN'T CHANGE

Four factors can increase heart disease risk. These cannot be changed.

Family history: You are at greater risk if close blood relatives have had heart disease.

Gender: More men have heart disease sooner in life. Women become more susceptible after menopause.

Race: Blacks have greater heart disease risk than whites because of higher blood pressure levels.

Age: Heart disease risk factors increase with age.

THE WORKING WOMAN'S HEART

When more women began working outside the home, researchers expected heart attack risk to increase significantly. With the exception of those who hold clerical positions, working women show about the same rates of heart disease as homemakers. It's not the work that affects the heart attack risk but the amount of control that women have over their work.

HEART WORKSHOP

To test your heart knowledge, take a few minutes to complete the true/false heart quiz.*

TRUE   FALSE

_____ _____   1. Men's heart attacks are usually more severe than women's and twice as likely to be fatal.

_____ _____   2. Pain in the left side of the chest is a sign of heart disease.

_____ _____   3. 40% of heart disease in American women is caused from being overweight.

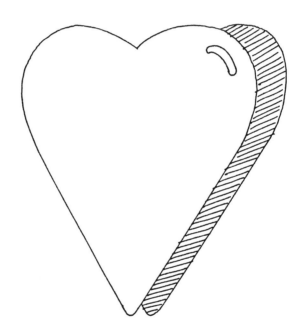

*Information source: American Heart Association

HEALTHY HEART STRATEGIES

You can help yourself to a healthy heart when you use these lifestyle strategies to control heart disease risk factors.

HEALTHY HEART STRATEGY 1. Don't smoke.

Women who smoke are two to six times more likely to have heart attacks than nonsmoking women. If you stop smoking for one year, heart attack risk is the same as if you had never smoked.

HEALTHY HEART STRATEGY 2. Check cholesterol.

Too much cholesterol is a major heart disease risk factor. Talk to your doctor about your blood cholesterol level. Avoid foods with saturated fats to keep your cholesterol level down.

HEALTHY HEART STRATEGY 3. Control high blood pressure.

Women with uncontrolled high blood pressure are three times more likely to develop heart disease. High blood pressure can't be cured, but it can be controlled with diet, exercise, and medication.

HEALTHY HEART STRATEGY 4. Control weight.

Get your weight into normal range and keep it there. Overweight women are more likely to develop heart disease, even if they have no other risk factors.

HEALTHY HEART STRATEGY 5. Exercise.

Your heart is a muscle and works better when it gets exercise. Inactive women have higher heart disease risk and poorer post-heart-attack survival ratios.

HEALTHY HEART STRATEGY 6. Manage stress.

Prolonged and excessive stress can create health problems. Women who feel out of control and have negative emotions such as anger, anxiety, low self-esteem, and hostility towards others are more susceptible to heart attack.

HEALTHY HEART STRATEGY 7. Limit alcohol.

More than two drinks per day can raise blood pressure, binge drinking can lead to stroke, and excessive amounts of alcohol can produce heart failure.

BREAST CANCER

VITAL SIGNS—Breast Cancer

- Only about 20% of breast lumps, bumps, and pains are due to cancer.
- When breast cancer is detected and treated very early, more than 87% of breast cancer patients are saved.

Thirty-year-old Jane is frightened. She has discovered a lump in her breast and will see her doctor tomorrow.

The good news is that the lump is probably not cancer. Lumps and pains can be caused by other common, noncancerous conditions.

Despite Jane's chances for a favorable diagnosis, breast cancer is a leading killer among American women. One in ten women will develop breast cancer in her lifetime. That's why a monthly breast self-examination should be a habit with women from their teenage years on. Most lumps are found by women themselves.

BREAST CANCER PREVENTION STRATEGIES

BREAST CANCER PREVENTION STRATEGY 1. Schedule regular examinations.

The American Cancer Society recommends that you have a regular breast exam by a health professional every three years from ages 20 to 40, and every year after age 40.

BREAST CANCER PREVENTION STRATEGY 2. Have a mammogram.

If you're 50 or older, you should have a mammogram (breast X-ray) every year. These low-dose X-rays often reveal cancer or a problem before a woman or her physician can detect it.

If you find a lump, swelling, tenderness, nipple discharge, or other breast changes, see your health professional without delay.

OSTEOPOROSIS

- **Half of women over 45 years and 90% over 75 have osteoporosis.**
- **A woman may have osteoporosis for 15 or 20 years before she realizes it.**

Sixteen-year-old Susie and her 40-year-old mother aren't aware that what they drink each day is putting them at risk of osteoporosis, porous bone disease that weakens the bones and makes them break easily. Susie is a typical teenager who likes to drink pop and very little milk. The phosphates in the pop reduce the ability of her bones to absorb calcium, the key mineral that prevents osteoporosis.

Susie's mother is a coffee drinker, and the caffeine in the coffee she drinks depletes the calcium she needs. People who drink three cups of black coffee lose twice as much calcium as those who don't drink coffee. Susie's mother could replace the 16 milligrams of depleted calcium by adding three tablespoons of low-fat milk to each cup of coffee.

OSTEOPOROSIS WORKSHOP

Women are eight times more likely than men to develop osteoporosis, particularly after menopause. Answer these nine questions to determine your chances of osteoporosis.

YES   NO

☐   ☐   1. Are you thin?

☐   ☐   2. Does your weekly routine keep you from exercising enough?

☐   ☐   3. Do you consistently eat few dairy products or foods with calcium?

☐   ☐   4. Are you a Caucasian woman?

☐   ☐   5. Did menopause occur before you were 45?

☐   ☐   6. Do you smoke?

☐   ☐   7. Do you drink a lot of alcohol?

☐   ☐   8. Do you have a family history of osteoporosis?

☐   ☐   9. Do you take medications such as corticosteroid?

If you answered yes to one of more of these questions, you may be at risk of osteoporosis. Like high blood pressure, osteoporosis is a silent disease. It happens when minerals and bone are lost over many years.

STRATEGIES TO PREVENT AND TREAT OSTEOPOROSIS

Consult your physician about following the five strategies that are recommended by health professionals for osteoporosis prevention and treatment.

OSTEOPOROSIS PREVENTION STRATEGY 1. Do regular, moderate weight-bearing exercise.

Inactivity leads to bone loss. Just about any exercise except non-weight-bearing yoga and swimming will help prevent osteoporosis.

OSTEOPOROSIS PREVENTION STRATEGY 2. Increase calcium intake.

Doctors recommend that premenopausal women have 1,000 milligrams of calcium daily, the equivalent of three and one-half cups of skim milk. Postmenopausal women should have 1,500 milligrams of calcium, the equivalent of five cups of skim milk, but experts agree that more research is needed about the role that calcium plays in osteoporosis.

Some women increase their calcium intake by supplementing their diets with calcium tablets. Some of these tablets don't disintegrate fast enough in the stomach to be effective. To test for disintegration, drop a calcium pill into a glass of vinegar and stir occasionally. It should dissolve in 30 minutes.

OSTEOPOROSIS PREVENTION STRATEGY 3. Get enough vitamin D.

We need vitamin D to absorb calcium. Women who get little sunlight exposure are at risk of vitamin D deficiency. Many calcium tablets contain vitamin D, but women should be careful not to take more than 400 I.U.'s per day because of dangerous side effects.

OSTEOPOROSIS PREVENTION STRATEGY 4. Discuss estrogen replacement therapy.

Your doctor may suggest estrogen during and after menopause or if both ovaries are removed. The decision about estrogen therapy needs to be carefully evaluated by each woman and her health professional.

Action Strategies and Resources

You won't just imagine 365 days of continued good health when you choose a lifestyle that embraces the vital strategies in this book. You'll become an energized working woman who can't wait to begin the day!

ACTION STRATEGIES

As you incorporate success and wellness plans into your life, remember these action strategies.

TRY ONLY A FEW STRATEGIES AT A TIME.

Make only one strategy change at a time. Don't try to do it all at once. You have made some winning decisions about your lifestyle, but it's easy to be discouraged if you try to initiate too many changes at the same time.

BE PATIENT.

Lifestyle changes are challenging and don't happen overnight. Give yourself time.

DON'T BEAT YOURSELF UP.

Some success strategies will work for you. Others will not. Don't be disheartened if one doesn't work. You can reap the benefits of others.

INVENT NEW STRATEGIES.

Be creative and you'll discover infinite possibilities for developing your own success and wellness strategies. The resource section of this book gives names of organizations and addresses where you can obtain additional information.

Who says you can't look and feel like a million? Get hooked on a healthy lifestyle. The challenge and the strategies are yours!

RESOURCES

ALCOHOL AND DRUG PREVENTION

National Clearinghouse for Alcohol and Drug Information
P.O. Box 2345
Rockville, Maryland 20852

Alcoholics Anonymous
General Services Office (6th floor)
468 Park Avenue South
New York, New York 10016
(or your local chapter)

AGING PARENTS

National Institute On Aging
DHHS
9000 Rockville Pike
Bethesda, Maryland 20892

Chapman, Elwood N. *The Unfinished Business of Living: Helping Aging Parents Help Themselves*. Los Altos, CA: Crisp Publications, 1991.

Video: *Eldercare: How To Help Your Aging Parents*. Los Altos, CA: Crisp Publications, 1991.

BREAST CANCER

American Cancer Society
3340 Peachtree Road, N.E.
Atlanta, Georgia 30026

National Cancer Institute
Building 31, Room 10A18
Bethesda, Maryland 20892

EXERCISE AND FITNESS

President's Council on Physical Fitness and Sports
450 5th Street, N.W.
Suite 7103
Washington, D.C. 20001

FINANCES

Consumer Information Center—R
P.O. Box 100
Pueblo, Colorado 81002

Card, Emily. *The Ms. Money Book*. New York: Penguin Books, 1990.

RESOURCES (Continued)

HEART DISEASE

American Heart Association
7320 Greenville Avenue
Dallas, Texas 75231
(or your local chapter)

National Heart, Lung, and Blood Institute
Education Programs, Suite 530
4733 Bethesda Avenue
Bethesda, Maryland 20814

NUTRITION

Food and Nutrition Information Center
National Agricultural Library
Room 304
Beltsville, Maryland 20705

Consumer Information Center—R
P.O. Box 100
Pueblo, Colorado 81002

OSTEOPOROSIS

National Osteoporosis Foundation
1625 Eye Street, N.W.
Washington, D.C. 20006

National Institute of Arthritis and Musculoskeletal and Skin Diseases
Office of Scientific and Health Communications
Building 31, Room 4C05
Bethesda, Maryland 20892

PREGNANCY

U.S. Department of Health and Human Services
NICHD
P.O. Box 2911
Washington, D.C. 20040

American College of Obstetricians and Gynecologists
600 Maryland Avenue, S.W.
Suite 300 East
Washington, D.C. 20024

SMOKING

American Lung Association
1740 Broadway
New York, New York 10019

Department of Health and Human Services
Office of Smoking and Health Services
5600 Fishers Lane
Room 1-10, Park Building
Rockville, Maryland 20857

STRESS

National Institute of Mental Health
Parklawn Building
Room 15C-05
5600 Fishers Lane
Rockville, Maryland 20857

National Mental Health Association
1800 North Kent Street
Arlington, Virginia 22209

VACATIONS

Volunteer Vacation Update
2120 Green Hill Road
Sebastopol, California 95472

WEIGHT CONTROL

Weight Watchers International, Inc.
800 Community Drive
Manhasset, New York 11030
(or your local chapter)

Consumer Information Center—R
P. O. Box 100
Pueblo, Colorado 81002

WORK ALTERNATIVES

Wider Opportunities for Women
1325 G Street, N.W., Lower Level
Washington, D.C. 20005

Association of Part-Time Professionals
Crescent Plaza—Suite 216
7700 Leesburg Pike
Falls Church, Virginia 22043

RESOURCES (Continued)

WORKING PARENTS

The National Association of Child Care Resource and Referral Agencies
2116 Campus Drive, S.E.
Rochester, Minnesota 55904

Conrad, Pamela. *Balancing Home & Career*. Los Altos, CA: Crisp Publications, 1990.

WORKING WOMEN

9 to 5, National Association of Working Women
614 Superior Avenue, N.W.
Cleveland, Ohio 44113

National Organization for Women
1000 16th Street, N.W.
Suite 700
Washington, D.C. 20036

NOTES

FOR OTHER FIFTY-MINUTE SELF-STUDY BOOKS
SEE THE BACK OF THIS BOOK.

FOR OTHER FIFTY-MINUTE SELF-STUDY BOOKS
SEE THE BACK OF THIS BOOK.

We hope you enjoyed this book. If so, we have good news for you. This title is part of the best-selling *FIFTY-MINUTE*™ *Series* of books. All *Series* books are similar in size and identical in price. Several are supported with training videos (identified by the symbol **ⓥ** next to the title).

FIFTY-MINUTE Books and Videos are available from your distributor. A free catalog is available upon request from Crisp Publications, Inc., 1200 Hamilton Court, Menlo Park, California 94025.

FIFTY-MINUTE Series Books & Videos organized by general subject area.

Management Training:

ⓥ	Coaching & Counseling	68-8
	Conducting Training Sessions	193-7
	Delegating for Results	008-6
	Developing Instructional Design	076-0
ⓥ	Effective Meeting Skills	33-5
ⓥ	Empowerment	096-5
	Ethics in Business	69-6
	Goals & Goal Setting	183-X
	Handling the Difficult Employee	179-1
ⓥ	An Honest Day's Work: Motivating Employees	39-4
ⓥ	Increasing Employee Productivity	10-8
ⓥ	Leadership Skills for Women	62-9
	Learning to Lead	43-4
ⓥ	Managing Disagreement Constructively	41-6
ⓥ	Managing for Commitment	099-X
	Managing the Older Work Force	182-1
ⓥ	Managing Organizational Change	80-7
	Managing the Technical Employee	177-5
	Mentoring	123-6
ⓥ	The New Supervisor—Revised	120-1
	Personal Performance Contracts—Revised	12-2
ⓥ	Project Management	75-0
ⓥ	Quality at Work: A Personal Guide to Professional Standards	72-6
	Rate Your Skills As a Manager	101-5
	Recruiting Volunteers: A Guide for Nonprofits	141-4
	Risk Taking	076-9
	Selecting & Working with Consultants	87-4
	Self-Managing Teams	00-0
	Successful Negotiation—Revised	09-2
	Systematic Problem Solving & Decision Making	63-7

Management Training (continued):

(v) Team Building—Revised   118-X
Training Managers to Train   43-2
Training Methods That Work   082-5
Understanding Organizational Change   71-8
(v) Working Together in a Multicultural Organization   85-8

Personal Improvement:

(v) Attitude: Your Most Priceless Possession—Revised   011-6
Business Etiquette & Professionalism   32-9
Concentration!   073-6
The Continuously Improving Self: A Personal Guide to TQM   151-1
(v) Developing Positive Assertiveness   38-6
Developing Self-Esteem   66-1
Finding Your Purpose: A Guide to Personal Fulfillment   072-8
From Technical Specialist to Supervisor   194-X
Managing Anger   114-7
Memory Skills in Business   56-4
Organizing Your Workspace   125-2
(v) Personal Time Management   22-X
Plan Your Work—Work Your Plan!   078-7
Self-Empowerment   128-7
Stop Procrastinating: Get to Work!   88-2
Successful Self-Management   26-2
The Telephone & Time Management   53-X
Twelve Steps to Self-Improvement   102-3

Human Resources & Wellness:

Attacking Absenteeism   042-6
(v) Balancing Home & Career—Revised   35-3
Downsizing Without Disaster   081-7
Effective Performance Appraisals—Revised   11-4
Effective Recruiting Strategies   127-9
Employee Benefits with Cost Control   133-3
Giving & Receiving Criticism   023-X
Guide to Affirmative Action   54-8
Guide to OSHA   180-5
Health Strategies for Working Women   079-5
(v) High Performance Hiring   088-4
(v) Job Performance & Chemical Dependency   27-0
(v) Managing Personal Change   74-2
Managing Upward: Managing Your Boss   131-7
(v) Men and Women: Partners at Work   009-4
(v) Mental Fitness: A Guide to Stress Management   15-7
New Employee Orientation   46-7
Office Management: A Guide to Productivity   005-1
Overcoming Anxiety   29-9
Personal Counseling   14-9
Personal Wellness: Achieving Balance for Healthy Living   21-3
Preventing Job Burnout   23-8

Human Resources & Wellness (continued):

Productivity at the Workstation: Wellness & Fitness at Your Desk   41-8
Professional Excellence for Secretaries   52-1
Quality Interviewing—Revised   13-0
Sexual Harassment in the Workplace   153-8
Stress That Motivates: Self-Talk Secrets for Success   150-3
Wellness in the Workplace   20-5
Winning at Human Relations   86-6
Writing a Human Resources Manual   70-X
(V) Your First Thirty Days in a New Job   003-5

Communications & Creativity:

The Art of Communicating   45-9
(V) Writing Business Proposals & Reports—Revised   25-4
(V) The Business of Listening   34-3
Business Report Writing   122-8
Creative Decision Making   098-1
(V) Creativity in Business   67-X
Dealing Effectively with the Media   116-3
(V) Effective Presentation Skills   24-6
Facilitation Skills   199-6
Fifty One-Minute Tips to Better Communication   071-X
Formatting Letters & Memos on the Microcomputer   130-9
Influencing Others   84-X
(V) Making Humor Work   61-0
Speedreading in Business   78-5
Technical Presentation Skills   55-6
Technical Writing in the Corporate World   004-3
Think on Your Feet   117-1
Visual Aids in Business   77-7
Writing Fitness   35-1

Customer Service/Sales Training:

Beyond Customer Service: The Art of Customer Retention   115-5
(V) Calming Upset Customers   65-3
(V) Customer Satisfaction—Revised   084-1
Effective Sales Management   31-0
Exhibiting at Tradeshows   137-6
Improving Your Company Image   136-8
Managing Quality Customer Service   83-1
Measuring Customer Satisfaction   178-3
Professional Selling   42-4
(V) Quality Customer Service—Revised   95-5
Restaurant Server's Guide—Revised   08-4
Sales Training Basics—Revised   119-8
Telemarketing Basics   60-2
(V) Telephone Courtesy & Customer Service—Revised   064-7

Small Business & Financial Planning:

The Accounting Cycle	146-5
The Basics of Budgeting	134-1
Consulting for Success	006-X
Creative Fund Raising	181-3
Credits & Collections	080-9
Direct Mail Magic	075-2
Financial Analysis: Beyond the Basics	132-5
Financial Planning with Employee Benefits	90-4
Marketing Your Consulting or Professional Services	40-8
Personal Financial Fitness—Revised	89-0
Publicity Power	82-3
Starting Your New Business—Revised	144-9
Understanding Financial Statements	22-1
Writing & Implementing a Marketing Plan	083-3

Adult Literacy & Learning:

Adult Learning Skills	175-9
Basic Business Math	24-8
Becoming an Effective Tutor	28-0
Building Blocks of Business Writing	095-7
Clear Writing	094-9
The College Experience: Your First Thirty Days on Campus	07-8
Easy English	198-8
Going Back to School: An Adult Perspective	142-2
Introduction to Microcomputers: The Least You Should Know	087-6
Language, Customs & Protocol for Foreign Students	097-3
Improve Your Reading	086-8
Returning to Learning: Getting Your G.E.D.	02-7
Study Skills Strategies—Revised	05-X
Vocabulary Improvement	124-4

Career/Retirement & Life Planning:

Career Discovery—Revised	07-6
Developing Strategic Resumes	129-5
Effective Networking	30-2
I Got the Job!—Revised	121-X
Job Search That Works	105-8
Plan B: Protecting Your Career from Change	48-3
Preparing for Your Interview	33-7